THE POWER OF YOUR PAUSE

by

Dr. Moniek Garside, Ph.D., LCSW

First Edition

Published by Mindful Media Group, LLC

Author: Dr. Moniek Garside, Ph.D., LCSW

www.moniekgarside.com

Table of Contents

INTRODUCTION

The Forgotten Pause

You probably cannot remember the last time you simply sat still, not because you were waiting for something, but because you truly meant to. Most of us fill every available moment with noise — scrolling endlessly through feeds, planning what comes next, worrying about what might go wrong, or working hard just to keep up. The world moves fast, and we have learned to move faster, believing that speed equals success and that stillness is a luxury we cannot afford.

I used to be just like that — caught in the rush, swept along by the currents of constant motion. Until one day I realized I could not recall what being present actually felt like. I felt disconnected from myself, as though I was living life from the outside looking in; a spectator rather than a participant. That sense of disconnection was heavy and subtle all at once.

In the work I do, I often sit in sessions holding space for people who desperately need to pause. I gently nudge them to create room for themselves, encouraging them again and again that they are worthy of that pause — that they deserve the experience of feeling truly present. It is not always easy for them, or for me. The culture around us rarely encourages slowing down. It whispers that to pause is to fall behind, to lose momentum, to be less than. Yet, over and over, I witness the profound shifts that happen when someone finally allows themselves to stop, even just for a moment — the relief that washes over them, the clarity that emerges, the deep breath of recognition that they are enough, just as they are.

After years of this work and my own personal journey, I decided to write this book to share what I have learned and to invite you into this practice, not as a quick fix or a checklist, but as a way of *being*. Pausing is not about adding something extra to your to-do list; it is about reclaiming something essential that has been lost along the way. Pausing is about meeting yourself where you are, with kindness and curiosity, and opening the door to a different way of living.

I have had more than a few moments where I had no choice but to sit still, listen to my own thoughts, find my voice, and sometimes even change direction. One of the most vivid of those experiences was a recent solo trip to the mountains — a first for me. I was intentional about choosing a place with little to no distraction, somewhere I could be truly alone with my thoughts and the natural world. I planned ahead, let loved ones know my itinerary, and made sure I felt safe, so that I could fully allow myself the space to reset. Three days surrounded by nothing but quiet and sky reminded me just how deeply a pause can replenish you. The stillness was not empty — it was full of life, of insight, of softness and strength. When you step away from the swirl of daily life, you can finally hear what lies underneath it all: the subtle currents of your heart, the quiet urgencies of your mind. That experience changed me. It was a reminder that pause is not about stopping your life — it is about starting a new way of living it.

Your pause may not look like mine, and that is perfectly fine. There are countless ways to create these moments. Sometimes it is a weekend away, far from the noise and screens. Sometimes it is a quiet cup of coffee before the world wakes up, when the house is still and the morning air is fresh. Sometimes it is just a few deep breaths between meetings, a brief stretch at your desk, or a moment to close your eyes and notice your body. What matters most is that it is intentional and that it is yours.

So, what does it truly mean to pause? To pause is to intentionally stop or slow down in order to create space for awareness, reflection, and choice. It is a conscious moment of interruption — stepping back from automatic reactions, constant movement, and urgency to observe what is happening both inside and around you. To pause is to hold a mirror to your experience without judgment, to meet your thoughts and feelings with openness rather than resistance.

Now, ask yourself: how often do you intentionally pause? Most of us only do it when we are forced to — when we burn out, when our bodies finally say, enough. The truth is, many of us are afraid of stillness. Busyness keeps us distracted from our reality. It shields us from discomfort, from uncertainty, from the parts of ourselves we might rather not face. But in stillness, you have the rare opportunity to sit with your truth — to discover the work that needs to be done, the feelings that need to be felt, the questions that need to be asked.

This book is an invitation. It is a starting point for creating pauses in your life some big, some small. Both matter. Both are necessary. And both hold the power to reconnect you with yourself and with the life you truly want to live. Pausing is not about escaping your responsibilities or retreating from your goals. It is about showing up more fully and intentionally choosing presence over distraction, clarity over chaos, and connection over disconnection.

Over the coming pages, you will find tools, reflections, and stories designed to help you build this practice. You will learn that pausing is not a break from life, but a way to live it more deeply. You will discover that the power of pausing lies not in perfection or grand gestures, but in the small, consistent moments where you choose to be present.

This journey is not always easy, but it is always worth it. The path to pause is a path back to yourself — a path to healing, to insight, and to a richer experience of your own life. I hope that as you move through these pages, you will begin to feel the invitation of pause, not as a distant ideal, but as a practical, living practice you can carry with you every day.

Welcome to the journey.

CHAPTER 1

The Science of Stillness

Stillness is not just about sitting quietly. It is much more than that. Stillness is a biological reset button — a deliberate and powerful way to let your brain and body recover from the constant noise, stress, and demands of daily life. When you pause, something real and profound shifts inside you, something measurable in your breath, your heart rate, and your ability to think clearly and with intention. This shift is not subtle; it is necessary for your mental, emotional, and physical well-being.

If you are reading this, I will assume you are at least somewhat intrigued by this journey. Good. Let us keep going.

So, what exactly happens in the brain and body during a pause? I will not dive too deep into the science, but I want you to understand its significance. A pause is not inactivity or laziness — it is regulation. It is a vital process that allows your nervous system to recalibrate. When we intentionally slow down, the nervous system shifts out of survival mode, which is all too often our default state of being.

Inside the brain, activity in the amygdala, our internal threat detection center, decreases. The amygdala is responsible for detecting danger and triggering the "fight or flight" response. When it is overactive, it keeps us in a heightened state of alertness, making it difficult to relax or think clearly. During a pause, the brain increases engagement in areas responsible for reflection, decision-making, and emotional regulation — primarily the prefrontal cortex, the part of the brain that helps us think clearly, assess consequences, and make intentional choices rather than react impulsively. In other words, pausing allows your higher brain functions to come back online, giving you the ability to respond thoughtfully to your life rather than being swept away by stress and habit.

In the body, the impact is equally profound. A pause activates the parasympathetic nervous system often called the "rest and digest" system. This activation slows the heart rate, deepens breathing, decreases muscle tension, and lowers cortisol levels, the hormone associated with stress. This physiological response creates a sense of internal safety, which is essential for insight, learning, and meaningful change. Without these moments of calm, the body remains stuck in chronic stress, unable to recover or find balance.

With pauses, the body receives a clear and crucial message: You are not in danger. You can slow down. You can choose.

To put it simply when you pause, you tell your brain and body that it is safe. You shift from "fight-or-flight" to "rest and recharge." Your heart slows, your breath deepens, and your mind begins to clear. You become less reactive and more thoughtful. This is where real transformation begins; not when you are rushing, but when you finally give yourself permission to breathe.

There is a pervasive myth in our culture that productivity requires constant motion. We live in a society that celebrates busyness to the point of exhaustion, equating nonstop activity with success. We are conditioned to believe that juggling multiple income streams, projects, and goals is the very definition of progress. It is everywhere we turn. From social media to blog posts, everyone praises constant motion. But the reality is that constant motion is not true progress. Constant motion wears us down in ways we do not notice at first. We become trapped in a cycle of distraction and a state of being overwhelmed.

Here is what is really happening: the myth of productivity tells us that slowing down is lazy, irresponsible, or even dangerous. Yet nonstop activity often serves as a form of avoidance and overstimulation. When we are constantly busy, we may be too distracted to feel, reflect, or recognize the unhealthy patterns quietly running our lives. Over time, this leads to burnout, poor decision-making, resentment, emotional instability, and repeated cycles of behavior we never intended to repeat.

True productivity is not about doing more. It is about doing what truly aligns with, sustains, and moves your life forward.

Pausing takes you off autopilot. It gives you something invaluable — space to ask yourself: Why am I doing this? Is this actually serving me? Without pauses, you miss key moments, important breakthroughs, and the reset that can quietly change the entire direction of your journey.

Science backs this up. Intentional stillness has measurable benefits for both mental and physical health. Research consistently shows that practices involving stillness such as mindfulness, quiet reflection, and slow breathing not only support emotional regulation but also reduce anxiety and sharpen focus. Stillness strengthens self-awareness by increasing the brain's capacity for insight and pattern recognition. It improves impulse control, allowing people to respond thoughtfully rather than react hastily. Over time, intentional pauses enhance resilience, decision-making, and clarity.

Physically, the impact is just as significant. Stillness lowers blood pressure, improves sleep quality, reduces inflammation linked to chronic stress, and supports immune function. Emotionally, it creates space for honesty — the kind of honesty required to take true ownership of your behaviors, boundaries, and choices. This is why the practice of pausing is so radically powerful, especially in a world obsessed with speed.

The pause is not a detour from growth — it is the doorway to it. In those moments of intentional interruption, you get to check in with yourself rather than simply check off the next item on your list. You have a chance to notice what you have been avoiding, to feel what is actually happening beneath the surface, and to recognize the patterns that may be quietly steering your life in directions you never intended.

Pausing is not about losing momentum. It is about making sure you are moving in the right direction.

When you pause, you reclaim your energy, your focus, and your sense of purpose. You open yourself to insight. You give your mind and body a chance to reset, to heal, and to choose rather than simply react. Sometimes, all it takes is a breath, a question, or a single moment of stillness to reveal a path forward — one that actually leads where you want to go.

Beyond the science, pausing is a radical act of self-care and self-love. It is a way of honoring your humanity in a culture that often treats people like machines. It is an act of quiet rebellion against the endless noise, the pressure to perform, and the fear that you are not enough unless you are constantly doing.

When you pause, you reclaim your sovereignty. You say: I am here. I matter. My well-being matters.

As you move through this chapter and this book, I invite you to challenge the myth that constant motion equals progress. Give yourself permission to pause not just when you are forced to, but as a daily practice because you are worth the clarity, the healing, and the breakthroughs that only stillness can offer.

This journey will not always be easy. You may encounter resistance, impatience, or doubt along the way. That is completely normal. But every time you choose to pause, you strengthen your capacity to live with intention and be present. You open the door to a life that feels more aligned, more balanced, and deeply satisfying.

Pause is a practice. It is a skill that grows stronger with intention and patience. Like any skill, it requires repetition and perhaps most importantly kindness toward yourself. Some days it will feel effortless and natural. Other days, it may feel like the hardest thing in the world. The important part is to keep returning to it, again and again.

Notice how your body feels when you pause the tension, the breath, the heartbeat. Notice how your mind shifts, the moments when clarity arises or when the noise begins to slow. These are signs that you are reconnecting with a deeper part of yourself a part that holds wisdom far beyond the noise of daily life.

In the stillness, you find your center. You find your strength. You find the space to make choices that reflect not just what you have to do, but what you truly want to do. This is the profound gift of pause — a gift you give yourself every time you stop long enough to breathe.

You do not need special equipment or a perfect setting to begin. You only need your willingness to stop, breathe, and notice. This book will guide you through understanding, practicing, and integrating pause into your life, and you will discover that stillness is not emptiness, but a wellspring of insight, strength, and renewal. As you move through this book, you will be gently building your own toolkit of pause practices. They are simple, practical ways to slow down, tune in, and respond with intention. Each chapter introduces new tools designed to deepen your awareness, calm your nervous system, and create space for stillness in your daily routine. Remember, this toolkit is not about perfection or doing everything at once, but about giving you a collection of strategies to turn to whenever you feel life feels overwhelming or your mind races ahead. Over time, these tools become second nature, helping you live with greater presence and resilience.

As you move forward, remember: this is your journey. Your pauses will look different from anyone else's. Honor what works for you. Be gentle with yourself when it feels difficult. And celebrate every moment you choose presence over rush.

Your pause is not a luxury. It is a necessity.

Using the power of your pause is where your true story begins.

CHAPTER 2

The Fallacy of "Powering Through"

Now, we turn to something equally important: the tension between powering through and knowing when to stop.

Before we go deeper, it is worth acknowledging how profoundly ingrained the mindset of relentless pushing is both in our culture and within ourselves.

Grit is celebrated as the driving force that carries people through obstacles and toward their goals. It is that inner voice insisting, "Do not quit," even when every muscle, every fiber of your being, is begging for rest. This determination can be a powerful ally, helping you overcome challenges that might otherwise feel insurmountable.

But grit has its limits. Powering through might feel like the go-to move when things get tough, but it is often more harmful than helpful. Pushing past exhaustion or emotional overwhelm can drain your energy, cloud your judgement, and even increase stress or burnout.

When pushing becomes the only way you know to move forward , without pause or reflection, it quietly chips away at your well-being. The endless grind, the refusal to slow down or rest, leads to an exhaustion that settles deep into your body and mind, wearing you down over time. What begins as strength can gradually become a heavy burden, making it harder to think clearly, feel balanced, or find joy in the very goals you are chasing.

Physically, this kind of unyielding effort invites burnout, chronic fatigue, and a weakened immune system. When the body is pushed too hard for too long, it begins sending distress signals that often go unnoticed until they become overwhelming. Sleepless nights and relentless stress wear down the body's natural defenses, leaving you more vulnerable to illness and slower to recover.

Beneath this exhaustion, the body's fight-or-flight response can become chronically activated as if your nervous system is stuck on high alert, constantly bracing for threats that never fully resolve. This state of sustained tension drains energy and makes it difficult to relax or feel safe, even in moments that should be restful. Muscles remain tight, breathing stays shallow, and the mind stays restless, caught in a loop of tension and hypervigilance.

Mentally, the toll is just as significant. Increased anxious feelings and a persistent sense of overwhelm often reflect a life lived at full speed with no room to breathe. The mind becomes trapped in a relentless cycle of urgency and pressure, where every moment feels like a race and rest feels like failure. This constant activation of fight-or-flight narrows focus to pure survival mode, shutting down creativity, calm, and clarity.

Over time, it becomes harder to think clearly or make thoughtful decisions. The very drive that once propelled you forward begins to feel like a weight pulling you under. Your internal dialogue may shift from encouragement to harsh self-criticism, adding quietly to the strain.

This is where the pause becomes essential not as a sign of weakness, but as an act of courage.

The pause allows you to step off life's treadmill, breathe, and honestly assess what your body and mind truly need. It creates space to notice the early warnings of burnout before they become crises. By pausing, you give yourself permission to shift from relentless pushing to intentional care, a shift that preserves both your health and your capacity to move forward with purpose.

The pause is a protective boundary. It is a way of honoring your limits rather than ignoring them, and of listening to yourself with kindness and curiosity rather than judgment or resistance.

Knowing when to pause and when to press on is a skill that takes time and practice to develop. It is rarely a clear-cut decision. The mind will often push for more effort; more hustle especially when goals feel urgent or the stakes feel high. That inner voice tells you to keep grinding, to push through discomfort, because slowing down might mean falling behind or losing ground.

But this is where self-awareness the very quality we want to cultivate on your journey becomes essential.

The need to pause often arrives disguised in subtle ways. It might feel like a fatigue that no amount of caffeine can fix, a heaviness pressing on your chest, or a restless mind that refuses to settle. It can show up as irritability over small things, a sudden disinterest in activities you usually enjoy, or a quiet creeping sense of dread without an obvious cause. These sensations are not random they are part of your internal compass gently nudging you to slow down and listen.

Recognizing these signs takes mindfulness and honesty. It requires you to check in regularly with yourself, sitting with simple but powerful questions:

How am I feeling right now physically, mentally, and emotionally?

What does my body truly need in this moment?

Am I moving toward my goals with energy and clarity, or am I running on empty?

The first tool I want to add to your toolkit is a simple "***check-in***". Take a moment to step back and ask yourself: "Is pushing through necessary in this moment?" Notice any tension, fatigue, or resistance in your body. This tool may seem small, but it will help increase awareness by connecting you to the present state of the moment instead of acting on autopilot. It creates space to choose a response that supports your well-being. You might push forward with clarity or take a pause to recharge and come back stronger. This ongoing self-inventory builds the awareness that guides your choices helping you decide whether to press forward with renewed energy or to step back and rest, honoring both your ambitions and your well-being. Over time, this practice strengthens your ability to respond with intention rather than react out of habit, supporting not just productivity, but sustainable, balanced living.

As you learn to recognize when to push forward and when to pause, something important begins to shift in how you understand strength itself.

Our culture often equates strength with sheer force the ability to keep going no matter what. But there is a deeper, richer kind of strength that embraces rest and recovery as essential parts of the journey.

True strength is not only the capacity to endure. It also includes the ability and the wisdom to rest and replenish. Rest is not simply a pause in activity; it is an active, intentional process of renewal. It is the time when clarity returns, creativity sparks anew, and resilience is quietly rebuilt. Without this vital cycle of rest, strength becomes brittle and unsustainable.

The pause supports this process by offering a deliberate break from the constant demands and pressures of life. When you allow yourself to pause and rest, you are not giving up or losing progress — you are investing in your long-term stamina. This intentional rest creates space for your mind to untangle complicated thoughts, for your emotions to settle, and for your body to heal and regain energy. It offers perspective — a chance to see your path more clearly and return to your purpose with renewed vision.

Redefining strength in this way shifts the narrative from endless struggle to balanced endurance. It honors the natural rhythms that govern all of life: effort and ease, action and stillness. When you embrace this balance, you prepare yourself not only to face challenges with greater depth, but to savor the journey itself appreciating the moments of rest as much as the moments of forward movement.

The relentless drive to push through obstacles is admirable but it is not sustainable. The most courageous act is often simply to stop, to pause, and to listen to what is really happening beneath the surface.

The pause protects your well-being, sharpens your awareness, and ultimately deepens your strength. As you move forward, remember that grit is important but so is grace. The grace to recognize your limits. The wisdom to rest when rest is needed.

Pause is not the enemy of progress. It is the foundation.

When you learn to balance pushing forward with taking pausing, you build a resilience — a strength that carries you not just through moments, but through a lifetime.

CHAPTER 3

Noticing the Noise

It is 7:41 a.m. You are standing in the shower, but your mind is already at your first meeting. Or maybe you are driving to work and suddenly realize you have no memory of the last five miles. Autopilot is efficient, but it is also sneaky.

Most of us are so accustomed to the background buzz: the to-do lists, worries, half-read emails, and mental checklists. We barely notice how loud it has gotten inside our own heads. Pausing is how we turn down the volume.

We live in a world that rewards constant motion and relentless thinking. We pride ourselves on multitasking and "staying ahead," but in truth, we pay a heavy price. When the mind is always racing, always planning, always anticipating the next thing, we lose touch with what is happening right now. Our senses dull. Our choices become reactions instead of intentions. We miss the subtle signals our bodies and emotions are constantly sending: hunger, tension, fatigue, excitement, even joy. In short, we are not present.

The noise is not just external, it is internal too. There is the voice that says you should be doing more: the worry that loops in your mind on repeat, questioning your decisions and if something was good enough. It is easy to think this is just the way life is, but it is actually a habit — a habit of distraction, avoidance, and sometimes self-protection.

Noticing the noise is the first step toward changing it. When you start to tune in, you may be surprised by how much is running in the background. The mind's chatter can be relentless, but here is the good news: awareness is powerful. When you notice the noise, you create a tiny bit of space. And in that space, you have a choice: Do I want to keep running this script, or is it time to pause and listen instead?

This chapter is about learning to recognize your own noise. What patterns show up when you are tired, stressed, or trying to avoid something? What stories play on repeat? Is your mind always jumping ahead, or replaying something from the past, or drowning in a sea of "what ifs?" Does your body feel like it is always moving, even when you are standing still?

The purpose of pausing to notice the noise is not judging yourself or trying to come up with a quick fix. Pausing gives you time and space to awaken to what is actually going on within you. The goal is not to silence the noise. The goals is to become aware of the noise and how it disrupts your peace.

When you notice the noise, you can begin to turn down the volume. You can start to choose what deserves your attention, and what you are ready to let go.

Try this, just for today: once or twice, stop and ask yourself, "What is the noise in my mind right now?" Make note of what comes up. Then take a breath. That is all. This is the beginning of reclaiming your attention, your energy, and your sense of presence one pause at a time.

Busyness is often valued over balance. Noise often manifests as busyness or the need to always be doing something. And busyness without balance comes at a high cost; one we do not always notice until it has already ballooned out of control.

Constant activity can be so loud that it leaves almost no space to process feelings, to reflect on the patterns shaping your days, or to ask whether your life actually aligns with your values. Over time, this relentless churn leads to emotional exhaustion, decision fatigue, and a growing sense of disconnection from your own life.

The truth is, unbalanced busyness is a form of avoidance. Kind of like a child plugging their ears when they do not want to hear what you have to say. Busyness keeps you moving and tricks you into believing you are being productive, but it quietly prevents real healing. You can be in motion all day, every day, and not actually move forward. Many people stay busy to avoid discomfort, to keep from sitting with grief, or to sidestep a hard truth they are not ready to face. But here is the thing: what you avoid does not disappear. It simply waits patiently and stubbornly until you are quiet enough to notice it.

The cost is not just emotional. The body keeps score too. Chronic stress shows up as tense muscles, persistent headaches, shallow sleep, and a feeling that you never truly recover. You may find yourself more irritable, your boundaries weakening, saying “yes” when you mean “no.” Emotionally, the price is just as steep as resentment builds, numbness creeps in, and the things that once brought you joy slowly fade into the background.

When busyness replaces awareness, life can look full and feel strangely empty all at once.

This is not an invitation to abandon your responsibilities or toss your calendar out the window. This is an invitation to start noticing the difference between being busy and being present. To recognize that you can be active without being frantic and that sometimes the bravest thing you can do is pause long enough to ask:

"What am I really running from?"

"What would it mean to let myself feel, even just for a minute?"

What is this moment trying to teach me?

Because real connection to yourself, to others, and to your life begins the moment you slow down and listen to what is actually there.

Most of us do not even realize when we have slipped into mental and emotional autopilot. You move through your day checking boxes, responding to emails, having conversations — yet barely registering any of it. You are not really present. You are reacting out of habit, doing what you have always done. It is efficient, yes but it is also how you get stuck.

On autopilot, the brain falls back on well-worn neural pathways — familiar mental ruts that feel safe but may no longer serve us. We repeat the same thoughts, emotional responses, and behaviors without ever stopping to question them.

You might notice yourself overreacting to small things, numbing out with busyness or endless scrolling on your phone, or getting lost in work. You may feel emotionally disconnected like you are watching your life from a distance. You may find yourself cycling through the same internal arguments and self-criticisms over and over again.

Autopilot can sound like that harsh inner voice: quick to judge, quick to feel guilty when you set a boundary. It is the constant "should" running in the background; the constant feeling that you should be doing more. It's easy to think that this inner critic is just a part of who you are, something you should be able to silence with enough willpower. But there is more to it than that — this autopilot mode has roots in your experiences and the ways you have learned to cope.

Autopilot is not a personal failure. It is a survival strategy, a way your mind learned to keep you moving and keep you safe, especially when life felt overwhelming or unpredictable. But what once protected you may now be limiting you. Living on autopilot may keep you comfortable, but it also keeps you from truly living. It keeps you locked in old habits, old patterns, and old pain.

Recognizing when you have slipped into autopilot is the first moment of reclaiming choice. You can seize your opportunity to pause, to get curious, and to ask: "Is this reaction, this story, this habit actually serving me or is it just familiar?"

You cannot change what you do not notice. But the moment you become more aware of your own patterns, you are no longer just a passenger in your life. You get to take the wheel. And that is where real freedom begins one intentional pause at a time.

Let us talk about inner noise for a moment. That constant mental commentary humming beneath the surface of your day. You know the one: the running stream of thoughts, reminders, judgments, worries, and what-ifs that is always there, quietly shaping how you move through the world, even when you are not tuned in to it.

The good news is, you do not need hours of meditation or a silent retreat to start noticing it. What you need are small pockets of attention; just a few honest moments here and there.

Try this: pay attention to your internal dialogue during the transitions in your day. Catch it when you first wake up, right before you respond to a message, while you are driving, or when the house finally goes quiet at night. Do not worry so much about the content of your thoughts at first. Instead, listen for the tone. Is your inner voice rushed? Critical? Demanding? Or simply tired? Sometimes it is on a loop, repeating the same old lines you have carried for years.

You can create brief check-in moments for yourself little pauses that help you step out of autopilot. Ask yourself simple questions like: "What am I feeling right now?" "What does my body need?" "What am I avoiding?" These questions are not about judgment or fixing something broken –they are about getting curious. They gently interrupt the cycle just long enough for you to notice what is really going on within.

Another practice to add to your toolkit is called ***"naming."*** When you catch yourself lost in thought, silently label what is happening: planning, worrying, replaying, criticizing. Just name it. There is something surprisingly powerful about this. Naming creates a bit of distance between you and the noise; a quiet reminder that your thoughts are experiences, not commands. They are not always true, and you do not have to obey them.

Awareness starts with listening, not fixing. The goal is not to silence your mind or force yourself to "think positive" all the time. The goal is simply to hear yourself honestly and without judgment. When you learn to recognize your inner noise for what it is, you create just enough space to choose something different. And that is where things begin to shift — not all at once, but one pause, one honest check-in at a time.

Noticing the noise is an act of self-care. It is the first real step toward reclaiming your attention, your energy, and your presence.

You do not have to quiet the noise all at once. You just need to notice it gently and honestly. Give yourself permission to pause, to listen, and to question what has been playing on repeat in your mind. Over time, those pauses add up. They create space for clarity, for intention, and for a life that feels more authentically your own.

The noise will always be there. But so will your choice to pause, to listen, and to respond with something new.

CHAPTER 4

The Pause as a Mirror

Have you ever sat alone no phone, no music, not even a book for just five minutes? Most people do not last that long. Discomfort rises quickly, bringing with it everything you have grown accustomed to avoiding. The thoughts and feelings you have been running from suddenly wash over you. You may feel heavy, uneasy, unsettled. But within that discomfort lies a kind of mirror; one that shows you what is really going on beneath the surface.

The pause, uncomfortable as it is, is where you meet yourself. And discomfort is where growth begins. Our natural instinct is to escape discomfort, to fill the silence with noise or activity so we do not have to sit with the imperfections and unresolved issues that lie deep within. But it is in these moments of sitting in discomfort that transformation takes root. The pause acts as a mirror, reflecting back what is hidden beneath the surface, giving you an opportunity to understand, accept, and move through the discomfort, rather than running from it or missing it altogether.

When you stop rushing and step out of autopilot, the pause reflects back your thoughts, emotions, and deeper truths. It reveals the patterns you have been repeating, the feelings you have been burying, and the stories you have been telling yourself that may no longer serve you. It is not always easy to face what you see in this mirror, but it is necessary to do just that if you want to grow.

The pause offers a rare chance to slow down enough to ask: "What is actually real right now?" Are you feeling anxious because of an upcoming event, or because you are carrying old fears? Are you frustrated by a current situation, or because you are still holding onto an old hurt? The mirror of the pause helps you separate past from present, reaction from reality.

The next tool to add in your toolkit is ***"journaling."*** In moments like these, consider journaling about what you are feeling or thinking. Set aside 5-10 minutes to write without censoring yourself. It does not need to be lengthy or polished just honest. This practice will serve you well as you move through this journey.

Stillness has a way of uncovering what we keep buried beneath the noise of daily life. When you are constantly moving, distracted, or busy, there is little room for the quieter parts of yourself to surface. But when you pause and allow yourself to be still, those hidden feelings and thoughts begin to emerge.

This can feel uncomfortable at first. The discomfort might show up as a restless mind, unexpected tears, or a sudden wave of emotion that catches you off guard. Stillness is the mirror you never asked for. And like any mirror, it simply reflects what is there. Perhaps you tucked these feelings away because they were too painful, too hard to understand, or just too inconvenient to deal with in that moment. They are still there, waiting. This is what the pause does. It holds up the mirror to the parts of yourself you have been too busy to look at.

Acknowledging what the mirror is showing you offers a safe space to meet these emotions face to face. It gives you the opportunity to simply be present to look inward, and acknowledge what is really happening beneath the surface. Over time, this practice builds a richer, more honest relationship with yourself; one that embraces complexity and invites healing.

In this way, stillness is not passive. It is an active, courageous choice to turn inward and witness what lies beneath the everyday noise. The feelings and thoughts that emerge are not burdens — they are gifts. They provide insight, guide decisions, and open pathways for growth that remain inaccessible when you stay distracted or disconnected. Pausing, taking time to be still, allows you to see yourself clearly and honestly.

Discomfort in stillness is like a visitor who arrives unannounced and uninvited. You may feel anxious or overwhelmed, sad, frustrated, or uneasy. Whatever form it takes, you must slow down and pay attention. With discomfort often comes self-judgment; that inner voice that questions why you feel this way, or tells you that you should be stronger, happier, or more in control.

Self-judgment is one of the hardest barriers to overcome in the "pause." It can sound like harsh self-criticism, comparison to others, or a deep sense of inadequacy. This voice often disguises itself as protection, trying to shield you from vulnerability or failure. But in reality, it cuts you off from the very compassion and understanding you need to heal.

Be gentle with yourself. Give yourself grace. You are worthy of this moment to pause.

Learning to face discomfort and self-judgment requires patience and kindness. It means noticing these voices and feelings without adding more fuel to the fire. Instead of fighting or fleeing, practice welcoming what arises with curiosity. Remind yourself that discomfort is a natural part of growth and not a sign of weakness.

When you meet discomfort and self-judgment with openness, they begin to lose their power over you. You start to see them as fleeting experiences rather than fixed truths. This shift creates room for acceptance, self-compassion, and ultimately, transformation. The pause becomes a space where you learn to befriend your discomfort and quiet the inner critic because healing begins not when you feel perfect, but when you see yourself as fully human.

Using pauses to honestly assess your current state is one of the most valuable gifts you can give yourself. When you slow down and check in, you create a moment of clarity — a chance to see where you really are, beyond the noise and distraction.

This kind of honest assessment requires courage. It asks you to face your feelings, your thoughts, and your physical sensations without filtering or minimizing. It means sitting with questions like:

"How am I really feeling right now?" "Am I tired or restless?" "What do I need in this moment?" "Am I avoiding something that deserves my attention?"

These questions are not meant to produce quick fixes. They are invitations to simply stand and face your truth and be present with your reality as it is.

This is also a great time to incorporate ***"check-ins"***, a tool previously introduced. Try setting gentle reminders throughout your day to pause and check in with yourself. These can be simple moments: a breath before you answer a call, a pause before starting the next task, a few seconds of stillness at the end of a meeting. Use these moments to ask yourself what is happening inside. Over time, these small pauses create a habit of being present, helping you catch yourself before stress or overwhelm take hold.

Practicing this kind of pause builds self-awareness and emotional resilience. You become better at recognizing the early signs of stress or imbalance before they escalate. You learn to honor your needs and set boundaries that genuinely support your well-being. The pause becomes a mirror reflecting your truth back to you — not always comfortable, but always necessary. It is the foundation for making choices that align with who you truly are, rather than who you think you should be.

During your pause, try a ***"body scan,"*** another tool to add to your toolkit. It is a simple yet profound practice for reconnecting with your physical self and gaining clues about your emotional state.

Begin by bringing your attention to your feet. Notice any sensations — pressure, warmth, tingling, or discomfort. Slowly move your awareness upward: your legs, hips, abdomen, chest, shoulders, arms, neck, and finally your head. At each point, simply observe what you feel without trying to change anything. Notice areas of tension, tightness, or ease. Perhaps there is heaviness in your chest, or tightness in your jaw. Maybe your shoulders carry a familiar weight.

By tuning into these sensations, you access a deeper level of understanding about what your body is trying to communicate.

Remember, the mirror is not there to hurt you or make you feel defeated. It is there to show you the areas that need your attention and the places that are asking for your care. When you know what you are working with, you can make a better plan to support yourself. That might look like scheduling rest, seeking connection, setting a boundary, or simply choosing to breathe more deeply throughout the day.

As you begin leaning into this practice of pausing and meeting what shows up in the mirror, start slow. There is no need to rush or push yourself too far beyond your comfort level. Pausing can feel vulnerable, and it is important to honor where you are right now. Even a few quiet breaths or a brief moment of stillness can begin to open the door.

Keep your journal nearby to support this process. The goal is simply to move what is inside your head onto the page throughout your healing journey.

This act alone can bring remarkable clarity and relief. As you journal, pay attention to themes that emerge; connections between your experiences, recurring feelings, or stories that offer valuable insight. And do not forget to acknowledge what is good. The pause is not only a space for facing challenges; it is also a space for recognizing joy, gratitude, and quiet moments of strength that often go unnoticed in the hustle of everyday life. It is easy to miss these blessings when life feels like a whirlwind, but the pause creates room to notice and appreciate them fully.

Remember, this is a gentle journey toward greater self-awareness and presence. There is no perfect way to pause. There is purpose in every part of this journey, even the uncomfortable parts.

Give yourself permission to explore this space with kindness, curiosity, and patience. The mirror will reflect what you need to see. And with time, you will learn to hold all parts of yourself with compassion.

CHAPTER 5

From Awareness to Accountability

Now that you have identified areas that need your attention, the next step is to do something meaningful with that information. Moving from insight to action is a crucial part of your pause — the moment when awareness gives you a way to accountability.

The journey to accountability begins with awareness. When you pause to notice your thoughts, feelings, and patterns, you open the door to understanding yourself on a deeper level. This understanding is powerful, but it is only the beginning. Real transformation happens when awareness leads to accountability — when you take responsibility for your choices and commit to acting in alignment with what you discover during your pause.

It is one thing to see a pattern or recognize a habit that no longer serves you. It is quite another to take that insight and turn it into intentional change. Self-awareness matters because it enhances your ability to make changes that go beyond surface-level fixes or reactive responses. It is within this space of conscious knowing that the shifts you hope for become deliberate and sustainable. When you understand yourself deeply enough, you are able to honor your needs, respect your values, and invest in your long-term growth.

This chapter invites you to move beyond simply noticing and into the deeper practice of awareness and accountability, offering tools and perspectives to help you make sense of what you discover during your pauses. The goal is to support you in taking gentle, realistic steps toward meaningful change — steps where you truly take responsibility for the things of which you are now aware.

Accountability is not about blame or judgment. Accountability is about owning your power to shape your life, even when doing so feels hard or uncomfortable. This practice requires patience, compassion, and persistence. Holding yourself accountable with grace and kindness while setting boundaries that honor your needs is an essential part of your journey.

Approaching accountability with compassion creates a foundation of trust within yourself. It is this trust that turns awareness into action and intention into lived experience. In this way, accountability becomes the vital bridge between simply knowing and living a life aligned with your values — a life lived with intention.

Building self-trust is a vital part of turning awareness into meaningful change. It does not happen overnight or through grand gestures.

Instead, self-trust grows steadily, step by step, through small acts of accountability that show you that you can rely on yourself.

When you commit to even the smallest intention — whether it is pausing before reacting, setting a boundary with purpose, or following through on a simple promise to yourself — you reinforce the belief that you are dependable and worthy of your own care. Each small step is a quiet declaration that your needs and values matter.

These incremental actions add up. They create a foundation of trust that supports you when challenges grow bigger or the path feels uncertain. Self-trust allows you to face setbacks with resilience, knowing that you can pivot and keep moving forward.

Be gentle with yourself in this process. Building trust does not mean being perfect or never slipping up. It means showing up again and again, forgiving yourself when you fall short, and learning from each experience. Celebrate the small victories. Recognize the moments when you chose to pause, to listen, or to act in alignment with your truth. These moments are the bricks that build a stronger, more honest relationship with yourself.

Self-trust is the backbone of accountability. When you trust yourself, you are far more likely to take actions that honor your well-being and support your growth. It is a practice of gentle persistence and steady commitment to your own journey.

Yet even with growing self-trust, you may still encounter resistance and self-sabotage along the way. These obstacles are not detours from your path — they are an essential part of it.

Resistance often shows up as hesitation, doubt, or a quiet unease when you try to step into something new. It is a natural response rooted in the brain's instinct to protect you from discomfort or a perceived threat. Self-sabotage can take many forms — procrastination, negative self-talk, or actions that quietly undermine your progress. You may begin to second guess your decisions or rely too heavily on the opinions of others. Both are signals that deeper fears or limiting beliefs are competing for your attention.

Understanding why resistance arises is important because it helps you recognize that these feelings are not signs of failure or weakness. But in fact, are part of the process. Resistance is a reminder that growth requires courage and that change often asks you to leave familiar patterns behind. This is where you learn to make peace with discomfort.

When you acknowledge resistance without judgment, you create space to explore what lies beneath.

Self-sabotage can also feel like an enemy blocking your way, but it is often your mind's misguided attempt to keep you safe protecting you from vulnerability or the unknown. Pausing gives you the opportunity to notice these behaviors without reacting harshly. With self-awareness, you can begin to gently challenge the stories and fears that fuel them.

Working through resistance and self-sabotage requires self-reflection and action. It is not about forcing change overnight or expecting a smooth, uninterrupted path. It is about showing up consistently, even when parts of you want to resist. Each time you pause and choose differently, you loosen the grip of resistance and build new, healthier patterns.

This is where the pause truly becomes a catalyst for transformation meeting resistance with curiosity rather than fear, understanding your inner obstacles, and responding with intention instead of reaction. It is through this process that you reclaim your power and move forward with greater clarity and confidence.

Once you have begun to navigate resistance with this new mindset, it becomes possible to channel your awareness into purposeful action. One of the most powerful tools for this is ***"intentionality."*** More specifically pairing a clear intention with small, manageable steps.

After pausing and noticing what is arising within you, whether it is a pattern you want to change, a boundary you want to set, or a value you want to honor, setting a clear intention gives direction to your awareness.

An intention is a simple, positive statement about what you want to cultivate or how you want to show up. It is not about perfection or achieving a specific outcome. It is about guiding your attention and energy toward what matters most. For example:

"I will listen to my body's signals today."

"I will speak my truth with kindness."

"I will take one small step toward my goal."

These are gentle, affirming commitments that invite you to return to what is important even when distractions or doubts arise.

Once you have your intention, break it down into small, realistic actions that feel achievable and compassionate. This might be a great time to check your boundaries. What boundaries do you have in place to protect the intentions you set?

By pairing intention with concrete action, you create a feedback loop that strengthens accountability. The key is to choose actions that honor your current capacity and meet you exactly where you are. Each small step reinforces your commitment and builds self-trust. It transforms abstract awareness into lived experience moving you beyond observation and into real, lasting change.

Remember, the goal is steady progress, not perfection. Celebrate each action you take, no matter how small. Over time, this practice of intention and action becomes a powerful habit one that bridges the space between knowing and doing, and leads you toward a life lived with greater purpose and presence.

This is a great time to use your ***"check-in"*** tool— a regular pause to reflect on how well you are honoring the commitments you have made to yourself. During your check-in, sit with a few key questions:

What actions did I take that aligned with my intention?

Where did I notice resistance or hesitation?

How did I respond to those moments?

What can I learn from this to better support myself going forward?

These are not questions for self-criticism they are invitations to explore your journey with curiosity and kindness.

Write your reflections in your journal. The important thing is to create a consistent space where you can honestly track your progress and hold yourself accountable with compassion and without judgment.

This practice helps you identify patterns, celebrate your wins, and notice where adjustments might be needed. Real-time course corrections keep you moving forward with both intention and flexibility.

This simple yet powerful ritual turns accountability into a compassionate conversation with yourself. It reinforces the connection between intention and action, deepens self-trust, and keeps you engaged in your journey with clarity and presence. This is your opportunity to learn from every step you take.

As you move into the next chapter, remember that awareness is only the starting point. True change begins when you take ownership of what you discover within yourself. Accountability is the bridge that connects insight to action — inviting you to step into your power with patience and kindness.

Resistance and self-sabotage will be challenging. But they are part of the process, not obstacles to your growth. Meeting them with curiosity rather than judgment allows you to move forward with greater clarity and confidence.

By setting clear intentions and breaking them into manageable steps, you create a practical path simple awareness to meaningful actions, turning your “pause” into purposeful progress. And by establishing a regular accountability check-in, you deepen your relationship with yourself, reinforcing trust, compassion, and realistic action along the way.

Change is a practice, not a perfect outcome. Every small step you take is a meaningful choice one that quietly shapes a life lived with intention and integrity.

CHAPTER 6

Growing in the Quiet

Having moved through the crucial steps of awareness and accountability, you have begun to create the space needed for real change to take root. Chapter 5 laid the groundwork helping you recognize patterns, set intentions, and take meaningful action. Now, with that foundation in place, growth begins to unfold in quieter, more subtle ways.

Personal growth often comes quietly, without grand announcements or sudden breakthroughs. It rarely announces itself with fanfare. Instead, it reveals itself in the stillness that follows the initial movement after you have done the work to pause, notice, and choose differently.

This next phase invites you to hold space for what is emerging beneath the surface. Growth deepens here not through constant doing, but through being present in the quiet moments that connect you to your inner world. In that stillness, you begin to tune in with increasing sensitivity to the subtle signals of your thoughts, feelings, and deeper desires.

Pausing allows insight to arise naturally, without force or pressure. Rather than chasing change or manufacturing progress, you begin to receive it as it gently unfolds like a slow dawn breaking through the night. This kind of growth often remains invisible to the outside world, but is profoundly felt within. It is the slow, steady stirring of transformation that carries the most lasting impact.

Trusting slow progress is essential in this phase. Change rarely moves in a straight line — it twists and turns, sometimes seeming to stall or even move backward. This can feel frustrating, especially when you are eager for transformation or find yourself comparing your journey to someone who appears to be advancing more quickly or effortlessly. Yet it is important to remember that meaningful change often unfolds gradually.

To trust the process means embracing the pace that feels right for you, rather than rushing or forcing results. It means honoring your unique rhythm and allowing shifts to emerge naturally, even when they seem small or insignificant. Each subtle adjustment, every quiet moment of choice, contributes to a larger unfolding that may not be immediately visible but deeply significant.

Slow progress is not a sign of failure or lack of effort. It is the careful cultivation of new ways of being habits, mindsets, and patterns that take root deeply and are built to last. This kind of growth is resilient because it is grounded in patience and presence.

Trusting slow progress keeps you committed even when the path feels uncertain. The most lasting transformation often happens beneath the surface, in the quiet and steady work of becoming. It is here that you develop endurance: the kind of strength that carries you through setbacks, doubts, and the inevitable discomfort.

In these quiet moments, you have the opportunity to nurture new habits and cultivate mindsets that support your growth. Intention meets patience here. Effort is balanced with grace. This nurturing is powerful because it aligns with the natural rhythm of change, honoring the quiet so that new parts of yourself can emerge fully, without rushing or resistance.

Growing in the quiet is a profound practice. It teaches you to trust yourself, to be gentle with your journey, and to welcome transformation on its own terms. Rather than forcing change or racing toward an outcome, this practice invites you to slow down and be present with whatever is emerging no matter how subtle or gradual it may seem.

In doing so, you build a foundation that supports not just change, but true evolution one that carries you forward with clarity, presence, and purpose.

Here is where we will lean heavily on journaling, but not just simple journaling. Try ***"mindful journaling."*** Mindful journaling differs from regular journaling in its intention and approach. Mindful journaling is more than simply recording your thoughts. It is a deliberate practice of tuning in to your inner experience with curiosity and compassion — a dedicated space to slow down, listen deeply, and engage with your thoughts and feelings without judgment or pressure to find immediate answers.

If you have not tried mindful journaling before, starting does not need to feel complicated. Begin by setting aside a small, consistent window of time five minutes in the morning, a quiet moment before bed, or a weekly check-in. Use whatever writing tool feels natural: a notebook, a journal app, or even loose paper. The key is to create a gentle routine that regularly invites you to pause and reflect.

When you begin, simply note what you are feeling in the moment. Notice any thoughts that arise without trying to analyze or change them. You might write about subtle shifts in your mood, insights from your day, or questions quietly lingering beneath the surface. The goal is not polished writing or problem-solving it is to observe and explore your inner world with kindness and openness.

Mindful journaling supports growth during the pause by giving form to what might otherwise remain vague or fleeting. It helps you track your experience over time, revealing patterns and progress that are easy to miss in the rush of daily life. Over time, it becomes a mirror reflecting your journey, showing not only where you are, but how far you have come.

By making mindful journaling a consistent part of your practice, you build a stronger connection to your inner voice. This connection grounds your growth in real experience rather than abstract ideas. It invites you to be present with all parts of yourself, the confident and the uncertain, the calm and the restless, creating a foundation of self-compassion that is essential for lasting transformation.

Another important tool to add to your toolkit is ***"grounding meditation."***

Grounding meditation helps anchor you in the present moment, reconnecting you with your body and breath. It offers a gentle, accessible way to settle the mind when the pace of change feels overwhelming or uncertain. Focusing on your breath or the sensations in your body, like the weight of your feet on the ground or the sounds filling the space around you, gently creates a calm, centered place within you. Being centered opens the door to reflection and deeper awareness.

For those new to grounding meditation, beginning is simpler than it may seem. Find a quiet place where you can sit comfortably without distraction. Start with just two or three minutes. Close your eyes if that feels natural, and gently direct your focus to the sensations of your body or the rhythm of your breath. When your mind wanders, and it will, notice this without judgment and kindly bring your attention back to the present moment. The practice is not about clearing your mind completely. It is about cultivating a steady, gentle return to the here and now.

Grounding meditation supports growth during the pause by helping you stay present with discomfort, resistance, or uncertainty rather than avoiding or reacting to it. This presence creates the conditions for transformation to unfold with less struggle, allowing you to meet your experience with curiosity and openness. It strengthens your capacity to tolerate discomfort and stay connected to yourself, even when change feels slow or difficult.

Central to both of these practices and to any meaningful growth is consistency.

Growth is not sparked by one-off moments of insight or occasional effort. It is nurtured through regular, repeated practice. Consistency builds a rhythm that supports the slow unfolding of change, making the quiet work of transformation a reliable and sustaining part of your daily life.

Each time you return to mindful journaling or grounding meditation, you reinforce your commitment to yourself and deepen the foundation of self-trust. This steady dedication allows new habits and mindsets to take root, becoming part of who you are, rather than fleeting efforts that fade. Together, these quiet practices create a compassionate inner dialogue, anchoring you in the present and building patience, resilience, and presence over time.

Through this steady dedication, you honor your unique pace and invite growth to emerge naturally supporting a transformation that carries you forward with clarity, intention, and purpose.

Take a moment now to pause and reflect. What quiet signals have you noticed within yourself lately? How might you create space each day to listen more deeply to your thoughts, your body, your feelings?

Consider setting a small, manageable intention to support this presence. Perhaps it is a few minutes of mindful journaling, a brief grounding meditation, or simply a mindful pause before responding to the world around you.

Growth is not a race it is a steady practice. Every moment you choose to slow down and tune in is a meaningful step forward. Honor where you are right now, and trust that in the quiet, transformation is already taking root.

CHAPTER 7

Bringing Pause into Relationships

As you have discovered in the quiet moments of your own growth, transformation often begins with a pause — a stillness that invites new perspectives and deeper awareness. This same principle extends beyond your inner world, reaching into the heart of your relationships. Just as growth within requires patience and presence, the way you connect with others thrives when you bring that same pause into your conversations.

Chapter 6 showed how stepping back and listening to yourself creates space for lasting change. Now, we turn outward to explore how bringing pause into your daily interactions can transform the way you communicate and the way you connect.

When you learn to pause before speaking, to listen deeply without rushing to respond, you open the door to empathy, understanding, and genuine connection. This deliberate slowing down reshapes not only what you say, but how you relate building bridges where there might otherwise be walls.

The pause is not just a quiet moment. In the heat of relationship dynamics, it is one of the most powerful tools you have. When emotions flare and reactions surge forward before you even notice, that brief stillness between what happens and how you respond offers a chance to breathe, reflect, and choose a path rooted in your values rather than automatic impulse.

That momentary gap is like a gentle reset — a way to step out of the rush and into a more mindful presence. It interrupts the cycle of impulse and reaction, giving your mind the space it needs to move from survival mode into thoughtful, intentional engagement. This simple pause carries a profound impact, turning reactive energy into honest dialogue and opening space for real understanding instead of conflict.

Pausing before you react is a quiet act of respect — not just for the person you are with, but for yourself too. It says: I am here. I am truly present. And I care enough about this relationship to choose my words thoughtfully.

I know it is not always easy, especially when emotions run high or when you just want to get your point across. But over time, this small habit builds trust and opens the door to conversations that feel honest and compassionate. That pause becomes a silent promise: I want to respond with care.

When you bring pause into your conversations, it gives you the chance to listen deeply — and I mean really listen. Not just waiting for your turn to speak, but setting aside your own agenda, your defenses, and the urge to jump in with your side. In today's fast-moving world, this kind of listening is rare. And it only happens when you slow down enough to make space for it.

Pausing helps you hear not just the words, but the feelings and needs underneath them. It changes the entire rhythm of a conversation, so your response comes from clarity and empathy rather than autopilot reaction. When you reply with intention, you honor the other person's experience while staying true to your own. This kind of mindful exchange cuts through misunderstandings and deepens connection, creating a space to be present where both people feel seen, heard, and respected.

Bringing pause into your relationships creates space where empathy can grow. Empathy lives in the quiet moments between words — in those times when you are fully present without rushing to judge or fix things. That space invites curiosity and compassion, offering a fresh perspective on the people you care about most.

Within that open space, connections grow and tensions ease, allowing each person to feel truly understood and valued. The pause becomes a bridge that carries you from conflict to respect and understanding, a foundation strong enough to endure. It is the place where walls start to fall and genuine connection takes root.

One of the most effective ways to bring pause into your conversations is through a tool called **"mindful communication."**

It might sound simple, but the moment you catch yourself about to react, whether it is a quick retort, a defensive comment, or a retreat into silence, stop. Take a deliberate breath and count to three in your mind. This small pause is like hitting a reset button, creating a crucial space to check in with yourself before words fly out.

Ask yourself: Am I feeling frustrated, hurt, feeling overwhelmed, or misunderstood?

Naming these feelings quietly to yourself helps you step out of giving an automatic reaction and into conscious choice.

Once you have tuned into your own experience, shift your focus to what you actually want to say and why. This is not about firing back or winning the conversation. It is about communicating with intention. What outcome do you hope for? Greater understanding? Resolution? Simply feeling heard and connected? That clarity shapes how you speak and sets the tone for the entire exchange.

Now bring your full attention to the other person. Listen without planning your rebuttal or letting your mind drift. Notice not just the words, but the emotions and needs behind them. When it is your turn, respond thoughtfully and with kindness honoring both your truth and theirs.

For example, instead of snapping back with "You never listen to me," you might say: "I feel unheard when our conversations rush by. Can we slow down so I can share what is on my mind?"

This shift from reactive to reflective changes the entire dynamic. It turns a potential conflict into an opportunity for deeper connection and mutual respect. Over time, this practice nurtures stronger, more authentic relationships built on understanding rather than assumption. It fosters an environment where both people feel safe to express themselves honestly, and to be met with kindness rather than judgment.

Another powerful tool is ***"reflective listening."***

Reflective listening is about showing the other person you are truly hearing them by summarizing or paraphrasing what they have shared before offering your own response. For instance, if a friend says, "I am just overwhelmed with everything happening at work," a reflective response might be: "It sounds like you are feeling really stretched by all the demands on you right now."

This simple act does two important things: it reassures the speaker that they have your full attention and that their experience matters, and it gives you a moment to genuinely process their words before reacting.

Reflective listening naturally slows the pace of conversation. It creates a rhythm that encourages openness and reduces the chances of misunderstanding or escalating tension. Instead of a rapid-fire exchange of points, the conversation becomes a shared exploration where both people feel seen and valued. In heated moments, this practice can be a lifeline.

Together, mindful communication and reflective listening invite you to slow down, listen with intention, and respond with care. They carve out space for patience and presence — the true heart of meaningful connection. When you bring this kind of attention into your conversations, you do not just talk. You truly connect.

Bringing pause into your relationships is not just about slowing down — it is about opening a new way of being with others altogether. The simple act of pausing before you speak creates space to be present and intentionally listen. It turns everyday conversations from reactive exchanges into meaningful opportunities for connection.

When you pause, you step out of autopilot and choose your words with care. You listen not just to respond, but to understand. You respond not just to be heard, but to build bonds.

This mindful approach softens misunderstandings and lays the groundwork for relationships that do not just survive but genuinely thrive. Remember, pausing is not silence or avoidance. It is a powerful moment of presence that transforms how you relate and connect with others.

The more you practice mindful communication and reflective listening, the more natural the pause becomes, and the richer your connections grow.

So, as you move forward, carry this practice with you. When conversations get tough or emotions rise, remember that the space you create by pausing is where true connection begins. In that stillness, you do not just talk — you truly meet the other person.

And that is where transformation lives.

CHAPTER 8

Making Room for Pause

Let us be honest: pausing feels inconvenient. It rarely fits the pace of modern life. We tell ourselves there is no time, that pausing is lazy, or that we will rest after just one more task, one more email, one more call, one more errand. But deep down, busyness often serves a different purpose. It becomes a way to avoid ourselves our feelings, our needs, and the quiet truths that linger beneath the noise and distraction. When we are constantly moving, we do not have to face discomfort, uncertainty, or the stillness that reveals what is really going on inside.

Making room for pause is not about magically finding extra hours in the day or blocking out large chunks of time. It is a far simpler yet profoundly more powerful act: choosing, moment by moment, to value your own well-being.

It means carving out small pockets of space where you can breathe, check in, and reconnect with what matters most. This could be a brief breath before answering a call, a moment to stretch between tasks, or simply noticing how your body feels in the midst of a busy afternoon. Making room means giving yourself permission to slow down — not as a reward, but as a necessity.

It is a way to build space for renewal, clarity, and presence. It is choosing to show up for yourself fully, rather than running on empty. And while these moments may seem small or fleeting, over time they create a foundation for greater balance, resilience, and peace amid life's demands.

Recognizing the importance of making room for pause is just the beginning. The real challenge — and the real lesson — is figuring out how to bring that pause into your daily life in a way that feels natural, manageable, and even nourishing.

This does not mean uprooting your entire schedule or carving out hours of time for meditation or retreat. It is about weaving small, intentional moments of pause into the fabric of your daily routines. These moments do not demand grandeur they ask only for your attention and a willingness to be fully present.

Start by noticing the natural transition points in your day. These are the little gaps that already exist but often go unnoticed the moments between meetings, the pause after a phone call, the short walk from one task to the next. Use these moments as opportunities to check in with yourself, feel your body, or simply rest your mind. Even a few seconds of mindful awareness can create space for calm and clarity amid the rush.

Throughout this book, you have been building a practical toolkit designed to help you embrace your pause and deepen your connection to yourself. The check-ins, journaling, naming, body scans, intentionality, mindful journaling, grounding meditation, mindful communication, and reflective listening deepen your ability to be present. Your toolkit supports your ability to respond rather than react, to choose presence over distraction, and to embrace the pauses as a vital practice that nourishes and fuels meaning progress on your own terms.

By embracing these simple strategies, you begin to reclaim your time not by adding more to your plate, but by creating pockets of space that support your well-being. Pause becomes less of an interruption and more of a steady rhythm woven through your life.

Today, notice three natural transition points in your day times when you move from one activity to another. At each transition, take a mindful pause. Close your eyes, if possible, take three deep breaths, and check in with your body. Notice any tension or tightness and consciously release it. Then set a small intention for what comes next.

This practice weaves pausing into your natural flow without disrupting your schedule. It is gentle, accessible, and surprisingly powerful.

Yet even with these benefits in mind, many people find themselves wrestling with guilt and resistance when it actually comes to stopping. That inner voice — the one that insists, "I should be working," or "I do not have time for this" — can be relentless. It is the echo of years, sometimes lifetimes, of messages that equate worth with productivity and value with constant doing.

You are not alone in this. Countless people wrestle with the feeling that taking a break means falling behind, being lazy, or failing in some way.

This inner critic is often rooted in perfectionism and cultural conditioning that glorifies busyness as a badge of honor. It can make you feel selfish for wanting to slow down, as if your needs are less important than the endless to-do list. These feelings are real and valid, and pushing against them can feel like fighting an uphill battle.

To move through this resistance, it helps to gently reframe pausing not as indulgence or weakness, but as an act of strength and self-respect. Rest is not something you earn after completing everything on your list. It is a necessary, ongoing practice that sustains you. When you begin to see pausing as a vital part of your success and well-being, it becomes easier to give yourself permission to stop.

Practicing self-compassion is key here. Notice when perfectionist thoughts arise and meet them with kindness. Remind yourself that you are human, not a machine and that your value does not depend solely on what you produce. This shift softens the grip of guilt and opens the door to making the act of pausing a regular, nourishing part of your life.

One powerful way to work through this guilt and resistance is to bring those difficult thoughts into the light and meet them with compassion.

Write down the exact thoughts that arise when you feel guilty for taking a break. These might sound like: "I am wasting time," or "I should be doing more," or "If I stop, everything will fall apart." Writing them down helps you see these thoughts for what they truly are just thoughts, not absolute truths.

Once you have them on paper, respond to each one with a compassionate reframe. For example:

"I am wasting time" becomes "Taking breaks helps me work smarter and stay focused."

"I should be doing more" becomes "Rest fuels my energy and creativity, so I can do my best work."

These reframes are not empty platitudes. They are reminders that pausing is not the enemy of productivity it is its foundation.

Keeping these compassionate reframes visible throughout your day on a sticky note at your desk, a reminder on your phone, or a card in your wallet can be incredibly supportive. They serve as gentle nudges to shift your mindset when the inner critic gets loud, helping you treat yourself with kindness rather than judgment.

The benefit of this exercise goes beyond changing your thoughts. It builds a habit of self-awareness and self-compassion that strengthens over time. Rather than fighting or ignoring the discomfort around pausing, you learn to hold it with curiosity and care. This creates space for new beliefs to take root beliefs that honor your need for rest as a vital part of your strength and well-being.

Creating a lasting pause practice means more than remembering to stop occasionally. It requires incorporating pausing into your environments both at work and at home.

At work, this might mean advocating for brief breaks during long meetings, helping to shift the culture toward recognizing that even a few moments of collective stillness can boost focus and creativity. You can also block out time in your calendar specifically for mindful moments five minutes of deep breathing before a new project, a short walk to reset your mind, or simply stepping away from your desk to stretch and release tension. These small rituals serve as anchors throughout the day, reminding you to come back to yourself amid the demands.

At home, building pausing into your daily routines can be just as powerful. Consider transforming familiar activities — morning coffee, meals, or bedtime — into intentional moments of rest and presence. Create physical spaces that invite pause and restoration: a cozy chair by a window, a quiet corner with soft lighting, or a favorite spot outdoors where you can breathe and simply be. These spaces become sanctuaries — signals to your mind and body that it is safe and welcome to slow down.

Communication plays a crucial role too. Let your family or housemates know the importance of your moments to pause. Frame them not as selfish or indulgent, but as essential tools that help you show up more fully and patiently for the people you love. When those around you understand that your practice of pausing supports your well-being — and by extension, your relationships they are far more likely to respect and support your boundaries.

Spaces that support your pause are not one-size-fits-all. They shift depending on the kind of rest you need.

For daily moments of quiet, these spaces can be small and seamlessly integrated into your normal environment — a corner of your desk with a plant and a favorite mug, or a cozy chair at home with soft lighting that invites you to sit quietly for a few minutes. These everyday pause spaces serve as gentle reminders to slow down and reconnect, offering quick breaths of calm throughout your routine.

For deeper restoration — those times when you need to step back more fully to reset and recharge — a change of scenery may be necessary. A weekend away at a quiet cabin, a long walk in a nearby park, or a dedicated retreat that takes you away from the usual noise and demands of daily life. These deeper pauses give your mind and body room to untangle and recover in ways that short breaks simply cannot.

Take a few minutes to identify or create at least two small spaces one at work and one at home that invite pause and calm. Add elements that support relaxation and presence: a living plant, a comfortable chair, a favorite mug, soft lighting. These details matter because they transform an ordinary spot into a sanctuary a place your mind learns to associate with rest and renewal.

Use these spaces daily as anchors for your pause practice. Over time, they become reliable touchstones you can return to whenever life feels overwhelming or your energy runs low. By cultivating these spaces thoughtfully, you create a foundation that supports both quick resets and deeper restoration — an essential balance for sustaining your well-being over the long haul.

This chapter rounds out the journey by inviting you to claim pause as an essential part of your daily life — not a luxury or an afterthought, but a choice you make moment by moment to honor your well-being.

With practical strategies, tools to overcome inner resistance, and intentional ways to build pause into both work and home, you now have what you need to sustain this practice long after the final page is turned.

Pause is no longer just an idea. It has become a lived experience the quiet power behind resilience, clarity, and connection.

CONCLUSION

Living a Life with More Space

This was never about perfection. It never was, and it never will be. It is about progress — a new relationship with yourself, built one pause at a time.

Every moment you choose to slow down, to breathe, to check in, you are reclaiming a piece of your own well-being. These small acts, repeated day after day, are the foundation for something much larger: a life lived with more presence, balance, and purpose. When we shift our focus from grand achievements to the simple, meaningful choices we make every day, something remarkable begins to happen.

Too often, we overlook the small victories in our rush toward the next big milestone. We measure success by finish lines and final products, forgetting that the journey itself is full of wins that happen quietly, almost unnoticed, in the spaces between our busyness.

Pausing is built on these tiny moments of choice. Those seconds when you decide to step off the treadmill, to listen to your body, or to simply be.

Celebrate each one.

Notice when you catch yourself before burnout. Notice when you take a breath instead of rushing, when you create space for stillness amid the noise. These are wins worth honoring because they are the bricks in the path toward sustainable strength and resilience. Recognizing and celebrating these moments keeps the momentum alive. It reminds you that progress is made in increments, not leaps.

It is the accumulation of these small pauses that builds a reservoir of calm and clarity enabling you to face life's challenges with greater steadiness. Each pause plants a seed of awareness that can grow, over time, into deeper understanding, compassion, and peace.

Pausing is not a one-time fix or a quick trick. It is a lifelong journey.

There will be days when pausing comes easily, flowing naturally like a gentle current beneath your actions. And there will be days when it feels impossible when the noise is too loud or the pressure too great to find even a single moment to breathe. There will be moments of clarity, when you feel deeply connected to yourself and the world around you. And there will be moments of struggle, when doubt and distraction cloud your path.

The key is to keep returning to yourself again and again, with curiosity and kindness.

This ongoing dance of pushing forward and stepping back deepens your connection to your own needs, rhythms, and inner wisdom. It teaches patience and grace, qualities that help you navigate life's complexities with greater ease. The journey of pause is, at its heart, a journey of coming home to your body, your mind, and your heart.

As you move forward from this place, remember that your pause is always available to you. It is not something you must earn or schedule perfectly.

Your pause is your secret strength. Your source of clarity and calm amid the chaos.

Embrace it.

Let pausing become more than an idea. Let it become a lived experience that supports you through every challenge and every triumph. Let it become the quiet thread woven through your days — present in the breath before a difficult conversation, in the stillness before a decision, in the space you lovingly carve out just for yourself.

Your pause is your power.

The journey begins with a single breath.

So, breathe deeply. Slow down. And step into the fullness of your life with intention and presence. The path is yours to walk one mindful pause at a time.

And as you walk it, may you find not only resilience and balance, but also joy in the simple, profound act of being here, now, fully and beautifully alive.

TOOLKIT REFERENCE GUIDE

1. Check-In ***(pg. 23)***

Purpose: We move through so much of our day without stopping to ask how we are actually doing. The Check-In is a simple pause — a moment to turn inward and honestly assess your emotional, mental, and physical state before moving forward.

How to Apply: Stop what you are doing and ask yourself one question: *How am I feeling right now?* Notice what comes up. Do not judge it or try to fix it. Simply acknowledge it, and then decide, with intention, how you want to proceed. This can take as little as sixty seconds.

2. Naming ***(pg. 30)***

Purpose: When we cannot name what we are feeling, emotions tend to run the show. Naming gives language to your inner experience and, in doing so, loosens its grip. It creates just enough distance between you and the feeling to respond thoughtfully rather than react.

How to Apply: When an emotion surfaces, resist the urge to push it away or immediately act on it. Instead, name it — out loud or quietly to yourself. "I am feeling anxious." "I am feeling hurt." "I am feeling overwhelmed." The naming itself is the practice. That is all it takes.

3. Journaling ***(pg. 33)***

Purpose: Thoughts left unexamined tend to circle. Journaling gives them somewhere to land. It is a tool for processing what is happening inside you, releasing tension, finding clarity, and beginning to understand your own patterns over time.

How to Apply: Set aside 5 to 10 minutes in a quiet space. Write freely, without editing yourself. This is not meant for anyone else to read, so there is no need to be polished or precise. Start with whatever is on your mind right now, and let the writing take you where it needs to go.

4. Body Scan ***(pg. 37)***

Purpose: The body holds what the mind has not yet processed. Stress, grief, anxiety, and even joy show up physically — often long before we are consciously aware of them. The Body Scan is a way of listening to what your body has been trying to tell you.

How to Apply: Find a comfortable position, either seated or lying down. Close your eyes and slowly bring your attention from the top of your head down to your feet. At each area, simply notice — tension, ease, discomfort, warmth. You are not trying to change anything. You are just paying attention.

5. Intentionality ***(pg. 44)***

Purpose: Much of our day happens on autopilot. We react, we rush, we respond — but we rarely choose. Intentionality is the practice of deciding, in advance, how you want to show up. It anchors your actions to your values rather than your circumstances.

How to Apply: Before your day begins — or before you enter a difficult conversation or situation — pause and ask yourself: *What do I want to bring to this?* Choose an intention: patience, openness, honesty, presence. When you feel pulled off course, return to it. That returning is the practice.

6. Mindful Journaling ***(pg. 51)***

Purpose: Mindful Journaling is writing as a form of presence. Rather than replaying the past or rehearsing the future, this tool invites you to write from right now — noticing your inner experience as it is actually happening, not as you remember or imagine it.

How to Apply: Before you begin writing, take three slow, deliberate breaths. Let them settle you into the present moment. Then write from that place — not from memory or worry, but from what is true right now. Notice what you are thinking, feeling, and sensing in your body as the words come. Let the writing be a way of paying attention.

7. Grounding Meditation ***(pg. 53)***

Purpose: There are moments when anxiety, overwhelm, or racing thoughts carry us far from the present. Grounding Meditation is a way back. It settles the nervous system and helps you feel stable and centered — not by changing what is happening around you, but by returning to what is solid beneath you.

How to Apply: Sit comfortably and take a few slow breaths — in through the nose, out through the mouth. Then bring your attention to the physical points of contact your body is making right now: your feet on the floor, your hands in your lap, the weight of your body in the chair. If your mind wanders, gently bring it back to those sensations. Stay here for five to ten minutes.

8. Mindful Communication ***(pg. 59)***

Purpose: To create a deliberate space between what you feel and what you say, so that your words reflect intention rather than impulse.

How to Apply: The next time you feel the urge to react — whether it's a sharp retort, a defensive comment, or a retreat into silence — stop. Take one deliberate breath and count to three in your mind. Use that pause to check in with yourself. Ask: *What am I actually feeling right now? What do I want to say, versus what do I need to say?* Then respond from that place.

9. Reflective Listening *(pg. 60)*

Purpose: Most of us listen while waiting for our turn to speak. Reflective Listening asks something different — that we truly hear the person in front of us. It is a tool for deepening connection and understanding, both in our relationships and within ourselves.

How to Apply: When someone is speaking to you, set aside the impulse to respond, fix, or advise. Listen fully — to their words, their tone, what they may not be saying directly. When they finish, reflect back what you heard before offering your own perspective. Something as simple as *"It sounds like you are feeling overwhelmed by this — is that right?"* can open a conversation that rushing past never could.

ACKNOWLEDGEMENTS

First and foremost, I want to thank God. Without divine guidance and grace, this journey would not have been possible. To my husband, Monty, thank you for always believing in my vision, for embracing my random projects, and for supporting my passion to lift others up. Your unwavering encouragement and love have been the foundation that allowed me to pursue this work with courage and joy. To my son, Mason, you remind me daily to lead with kindness. Your boundless love and gentle spirit inspire me in ways words cannot fully capture. You are a constant source of light and motivation. I want to express my heartfelt gratitude to my family and friends who have shown up in countless ways, cheering me on and holding space when I needed it most. Your presence and belief have carried me through the challenges and celebrations alike. To those who have allowed me to hold space for them, thank you for trusting me with the most vulnerable parts of your lives. It is an honor to walk alongside you and witness your courage and growth. Your stories have shaped this work and enriched my own journey. Finally, to everyone who has been a part of my team in any capacity, thank you. Whether through support, guidance, spontaneous calls, or quiet reassurance, your contributions have meant more than I can say. This book is as much yours as it is mine.

www.ingramcontent.com/pod-product-compliance
Lightning Source LLC
LaVergne TN
LVHW010118170826
845678LV00012B/2481

* 9 7 9 8 9 9 5 5 4 0 3 0 4 *